To:

_____

From:

_____

My Grandmother Showed Me the Stars

Illustrated by Becky Kelly

Written by Patrick Regan

**Andrews McMeel
Publishing, LLC**

Kansas City

08 09 10 11 EPB 10 9 8 7 6 5 4 3 2

ISBN 13: 978-0-7407-6370-0
ISBN 10: 0-7407-6370-9

www.andrewsmcmeel.com
www.beckykelly.com

Illustrations by Becky Kelly
Design by Stephanie R. Farley
Edited by Polly Blair and Jean Lucas
Production by Elizabeth Nuelle

My Grandmother
Showed Me the Stars

When I was very young,
I knew only of my parents.
They were the sun of my morning
and the moon of my night.

But when I first held my grandmother's hand,
I learned that love does not come from one source alone.

For Anna K. and her grandma

My grandmother looked into my eyes,
and I learned to trust.

My grandmother spoke softly to me,
and I learned tenderness.

My grandmother showed me that wisdom comes with age . . .

but that a joyful heart is forever young.

Days spent with my grandmother
seemed sprinkled with stardust,

with long games of Hearts
and raspberry tarts,

wandering walks
and "old days" talks.

She had the best clothes for playing dress-up,

the best garden for watching butterflies,

and the best-ever lap for reading stories.

My grandmother seemed to know everything—
even things that most adults have forgotten—
like where the fairies live in the woods . . .

and how to make lemonade with real lemons.

My grandmother showed me that you can laugh
and still be ladylike,

and be proud without being vain.

My grandmother told me stories
of when she was a little girl . . .
and I thought we could have been wonderful friends.

And when I got a little older, I realized that we were.

My grandmother showed me the stars—

and she taught me that each generation
casts lingering light on those who follow.

And, even today, no star shines brighter than my grandmother.